THE — POWER OF PROFITABILITY

Boosting Interior Product Sales in **90 days**

THE
POWER OF PROFITABILITY

Boosting Interior Product Sales in **90 days**

VIKAS ARORA

Worldwide Published by

Pendown Press

PENDOWN PRESS LLP

An ISO 9001 & ISO 14001 Certified Co.

Regd. Office 3767A, Kanhaiya Nagar,
Tri Nagar, Delhi-110035
Ph.: 8180886000, 9650072927, 8595249536
E-mail: info@pendownpress.com
Branch Office 1A/2A, 20, Hari Sadan, Ansari Road,
Daryaganj, New Delhi-110002
Ph.: 011-45794768
Website: PendownPress.com

First Edition: 2023

ISBN: 978-93-5554-609-8

Layout and Cover Designed by Pendown Graphics Team
Printed and Bound in India by Thomson Press India Ltd.

Contents

Acknowledgement

I would like to take this opportunity to express my deepest gratitude and appreciation to the individuals who have played a significant role in the creation and realization of this book.

Their unwavering support, encouragement, and belief in my abilities have been instrumental in bringing this project to fruition.

First and foremost, I want to express my heartfelt thanks to my parents, who have been my constant source of inspiration throughout my life. Their unconditional love, guidance, and encouragement have shaped me into the person I am today. Without their unwavering support, this book would not have been possible.

To my loving wife Pooja, your belief in me and your unwavering support have been a constant source of strength throughout this journey. Your patience, understanding, and encouragement have helped me stay focused and motivated during challenging times. Thank you for always being my rock.

I am immensely grateful to my daughter Gauri, whose innocent enthusiasm and love for storytelling reminded me of the power of imagination. You are my little ray of sunshine, and I am grateful for your presence in my life.

I would also like to extend my heartfelt appreciation to my channel partners such as Jain Interior Jaipur, Sunrez Interior Ahmedabad, Greenish Décor Chandigarh, Sethi Textile Chandigarh, SK Décor Nagpur, SR Industries Guwahati. Your trust in my expertise and your encouragement to embark on this writing journey have been invaluable. Your insights, feedback, and support have enriched this book and made it more relevant to the challenges faced by interior product dealers. Together, we can make a significant impact on their profitability and inventory management.

Finally, I want to express my deepest gratitude to all the interior product dealers who strive every day to make their businesses successful. This book is dedicated to you, as it aims to provide you with the knowledge, strategies, and insights needed to overcome the obstacles you face and achieve sustainable profitability. It is my sincere hope that this book will empower you to transform your businesses and reach new heights.

In conclusion, I am humbled and grateful to everyone who has contributed to this book, directly or indirectly. Your support, belief, and encouragement have been the driving forces behind its creation. Thank you from the bottom of my heart.

I am thankful to my friend Dinesh Verma, CEO, Pendown Press and his team for their support and suggestions throughout the creative process.

Chapter 1

Assessing
Your Current Business Model

1.1 Evaluating Your Current Revenue Streams

Assessing your current revenue streams is the first step towards boosting your interior product retailer revenue. This section will provide guidance on evaluating your existing sources of revenue to gain a clear understanding your business's position.

1.1.1 Reviewing Revenue Sources

Start by identifying all the avenues through which your business generates revenue. This could encompass sales from your physical store, e-commerce platform, wholesale partnerships, or any other sources. Evaluate each revenue stream separately and assess its contribution to your overall revenue.

1.1.2 Analyzing Revenue Performance

Once you have identified your various sources of revenue, analyze their performance using key metrics such as sales volume, profit margins, and customer acquisition costs. Determine which revenue streams are performing strongly and which ones may need improvement. Look for recurring patterns and trends that can offer provide valuable insights into your business's revenue generation.

1.1.3 Identifying Profitable and Underperforming Products/ Services

Evaluate the profitability of your product or service offerings across each revenue stream. Identify your best-selling products/ services, taking into account their profit margins, and customer demand. Similarly, recognize any underperforming products/ services that may necessitate adjustments or strategic changes.

1.2 Identifying Areas for Revenue Improvement

Once you have assessed your current revenue streams, it's time to identify areas for revenue improvement. This section will help you identify potential opportunities to enhance revenue and optimize profitability.

1.2.1 Market Research and Customer Insights

Perform comprehensive market research to gain a thorough understanding of current industry trends, customer preferences, and emerging opportunities. Analyze customer feedback, conduct surveys, and monitor social media channels to gain insights into your target market's needs and desires. Identify gaps in the market that align with your capabilities and have the potential to drive revenue growth.

1.2.2 Pricing and Profitability Analysi

Evaluate your pricing strategy and profit margins for each product or service. Assess whether your pricing aligns with the value you offer and whether there is room for adjustment to increase profitability. Consider conducting competitor analysis to ensure your pricing remains competitive in the market.

1.2.3 Upselling and Cross-Selling Opportunities

Discover potential opportunities to upsell and cross-sell products or services to your existing customer base. Analyze your customer data to gain insights into their purchasing behaviors and preferences, enabling you to suggest complementary items or encourage upgrades. Implement effective sales techniques to capitalize on these opportunities and increase your revenue per customer.

1.3 Setting Revenue Goals for the Next 90 Days

To stimulate revenue growth, it's crucial to establish specific and achievable goals. This section will guide you through the process of setting revenue goals for the upcoming 90 days, offering a clear direction for your business.

1.3.1 Assessing Current Financial Performance

Review your financial statements and assess your current revenue and profit figures. Analyze the year-over-year or month-over-month growth to understand your business's historical performance. This analysis will serve as a benchmark for setting realistic revenue goals.

1.3.2 SMART Goal Setting

Utilize the SMART goal-setting framework (Specific, Measurable, Achievable, Relevant, Time-bound) to set revenue goals that are specific, measurable, and aligned with your business objectives. Divide your revenue goals into smaller, manageable targets for the next 90 days. Strive to set goals that are both challenging and attainable, motivating and driving your team towards success.

1.3.3 Developing Action Plans

Create detailed action plans outlining the strategies and tactics you will utilize to achieve your revenue goals. Assign specific responsibilities to team members, set deadlines, and define key performance indicators (KPIs) to monitor progress. Regularly review and adjust your action plans as needed to stay on track.

Chapter 2

Optimizing Product Selection & Inventory Management

2.1 Analyzing Product Performance and Profitability

Analyzing the performance and profitability of your products is mandatory for optimizing revenue in your product retail business. In this section, we will explore the approaches to assess the success of your product offerings and make well-known decisions to maximize profitability.

2.1.1 Sales Data Analysis

Leverage your sales data to assess the performance of each product available in your inventory. Analyze metrics such as sales volume, revenue generated, and profit margins for individual products. Identify the top-performing products that contribute significantly to your revenue and profitability.

2.1.2 Cost Analysis

Perform a comprehensive cost analysis of your products, including production or acquisition costs, overhead expenses, and other related expenses. Make a comparison between the the costs and the sales data to determine the profitability of each product. Identify the products having low profit margins or are generating losses.

2.1.3 Pareto Principle (80/20 Rule)

Apply the Pareto Principle, also known as the 80/20 rule, to pick out the products that generate the majority of your revenue. Determine the top 20% of products that account for 80% of your sales and focus on optimizing their performance and profitability. Consider optimizing resource allocation by streamlining or discontinuing low-performing products.

2.2 Identifying High-demand Products and Trends

Identifying high-demand products and staying abreast of industry trends is crucial for attracting customers and maximizing sales. This section will provide guidance on recognizing market demands and leveraging emerging trends for your advantage.

2.2.1 Market Research

Conduct thorough market research to identify latest trends, consumer preferences, and demands specific to the interior product retail industry. Stay updated regarding the latest design styles, materials, and product categories that are becoming highly popular. Utilize market reports, customer surveys, and competitor analysis to gather valuable insights.

2.2.2 Customer Feedback and Reviews

Engage with your customers to gather feedback on their preferences and experiences with your products. Take advantage of customer reviews, comments, and social media interactions to identify high-demand products that are receiving positive feedback. Explore the possibility of implementing customer feedback systems to capture valuable insights for future product selection.

2.2.3 Supplier Partnerships

Develop strong relationships with reliable suppliers who can provide you with a diverse range of high-quality and in-demand products. Regularly communicate with suppliers to stay updated about the upcoming trends and new product releases. Collaborate with suppliers to ensure you have access to products that align with evolving demands of customers.

2.3 Implementing Effective Inventory Management Strategies

Efficient inventory management is vital for optimizing cash flow, minimizing costs, and meeting customer demands. This section will explore strategies to streamline your inventory management processes and ensure you have the right products available at the appropriate time.

2.3.1 Demand Forecasting

Utilize historical sales data, market trends, and customer insights to forecast demand for your products accurately. This will enable you to anticipate future demand fluctuations, minimize excess inventory, and prevent stockouts. Implement effective demand forecasting techniques such as trend analysis, seasonality adjustments, and data-driven forecasting models.

2.3.2 Just-in-Time (JIT) Inventory Management

Implement a just-in-time inventory management system to reduce inventory holding costs and optimize cash flow. Coordinate with suppliers to receive products when they are needed, effectively minimizing excess inventory and storage expenses. Ensure efficient communication and collaboration with suppliers to establish a reliable supply chain.

2.3.3 Inventory Tracking and Monitoring

Utilize inventory management software or systems to track and observe inventory levels, sales velocity, and replenishment needs. Set up automated notifications for low stock levels and reorder points to avoid stockouts and lost sales. Review inventory reports on regular basis to identify slow-moving or obsolete items and take the required action.

2.3.4 Strategic Pricing and Promotions

Optimize pricing strategies and implement targeted promotions to effectively manage the inventory. Utilize pricing techniques such as dynamic pricing, bundling, or volume discounts to stimulate sales and move inventory efficiently. Monitor the performance of pricing and promotional strategies to ensure they align with your revenue goals.

Conclusion

Optimizing product selection and implementing effective inventory management strategies are crucial for boosting revenue in the interior product retail industry. By analyzing product performance, identifying high-demand products and trends, and streamlining inventory management processes, you can maximize profitability, improve customer satisfaction, and drive revenue growth. It is important to regularly assess and adapt your product selection and inventory management strategies to remain aligned with market dynamics and customer preferences.

Chapter 3

Enhancing Store Layout & Visual Merchandising

A well-designed store layout and effective visual merchandising techniques play a crucial role in attracting customers, boosting sales, and enhancing the overall shopping experience. In this chapter, we will explore strategies to create an appealing store layout, leverage visual merchandising techniques, and optimize product placement for cross-selling opportunities.

3.1 Creating an Appealing and Customer-Friendly Store Layout

3.1.1 Understanding Customer Flow

Analyze the flow of customer traffic within your store to identify areas with high footfall and determine the optimal placement for key product categories. Consider factors such as entry points, aisle widths, and checkout locations to create a seamless and customer- focused store layout.

3.1.2 Zoning and Segmentation

Divide your store into distinct zones or departments to guide customers through their shopping journey. Allocate dedicated areas for different product categories or themes, enabling logical and intuitive navigation. Strategically place high-margin or high-demand products to capture customers' attention.

3.1.3 Optimal Use of Space

Maximize the use of available space by implementing effective space planning techniques. Balance open areas with product displays to create an inviting atmosphere. Ensure that the aisles are wide enough to accommodate smooth customer flow and provide ample space for browsing and exploration.

3.2 Utilizing Visual Merchandising Techniques to Boost Sales

3.2.1 Window Displays: Create eye-catching window displays that showcase your most attractive and desirable products. Use creative props, strategic lighting and entice them into your store. Keep your window displays fresh to align with seasonal trends or promotions.

3.2.2 Signage and Graphics

Utilize clear and informative signage throughout your store to guide customers and highlight key product features or promotions. Use visually appealing graphics, colors, and typography to convey your brand identity and create a cohesive visual experience.

3.2.3 Product Placement and Grouping

Strategically position products to encourage exploration and boost sales. Group complementary items together to facilitate cross-selling opportunities. Create focal points or feature areas to showcase new arrivals or high-margin products that capture customer attention.

3.2.4 Lighting and Ambiance

Optimize lighting to create a welcoming and engaging ambience. Use a combination of ambient, accent, and task lighting to highlight products and create a sense of warmth and comfort. Adjust lighting levels for different areas accordingly and product displays.

3.3 Optimizing Product Placement and Cross-Selling Opportunities

3.3.1 Point-of-Purchase Displays

Strategically position point-of-purchase displays near checkout counters to encourage impulse purchases. Highlight small, affordable items or last-minute deals to capitalize on customers' inclination for additional purchases.

3.3.2 Cross-Selling Strategies

Identify cross-selling opportunities by placing complementary products in close proximity to each other. Create displays or signage that suggest related items or offer package deals. Train your sales staff to actively engage customers and recommend additional products based on their needs and preferences.

3.3.3 Test and Measure

Regularly test different product placement strategies and visual merchandising techniques. Monitor sales data and gather customer feedback to assess the effectiveness of your efforts. Adjust and refine your displays and placements based on the insights derived from testing.

Conclusion

Enhancing your store layout and implementing effective visual merchandising techniques can have a profound impact on your interior product retailer revenue. By creating an appealing and customer-friendly store layout, utilizing visual merchandising strategies to boost sales, and optimizing product placement for cross-selling opportunities, you can enhance the shopping experience, augment customer engagement, and drive increased. It is mandatory to consistently evaluate and adjust your store layout and visual merchandising strategies based on customer feedback and sales data to remained competitive in the ever-growing retail landscape.

Chapter 4

Developing a Compelling
Online Presence

In today's digital era, developing a compelling online presence is essential for interior product retailers to reach a wider audience, attract customers, and boost revenue. This chapter will guide you through the process of building an engaging website, leveraging social media and digital marketing channels, and implementing effective online sales and promotion strategies.

4.1 Building an Engaging and User-Friendly Website

4.1.1 Clear Branding and Design

Make sure your website reflects your brand identity by integrating consistent branding elements such as logos, color schemes, and typography. Create a visually appealing and polished design that resonates with the preference of your target market. Moreover, make sure your website is responsive and mobile-friendly for a seamless user experience across various devices.

4.1.2 Intuitive Navigation and User Experience

Design your website with clear and user-friendly navigation menus that enable visitors to easily find products, information, and contact details. Optimize the user experience by reducing load times, providing high-quality product images, and incorporating user-friendly features such as search functionality and filters.

4.1.3 Compelling Product Descriptions and Visuals:

Craft compelling and detailed product descriptions that highlight the unique features, benefits, and applications of your interior products. Include high-resolution images, videos, or 360-degree product views to provide clear understanding of the product's appearance and quality to the customers.

4.1.4 Seamless Checkout Process

Simplify the checkout process by minimizing the number of steps and creating a secure and user-friendly payment gateway. Provide multiple payment options and be transparent regarding the shipping and return policies to build trust and reduce cart abandonment rates.

4.2 Leveraging Social Media and Digital Marketing Channels

4.2.1 Social Media Presence

Establish a strong presence on suitable social media platforms such as Instagram, Facebook, Pinterest, or Houzz, depending on your target audience. Post engaging content, including product showcases, design inspiration, and customer testimonials regularly. Interact with your followers, respond to their comments, and actively engage with industry influencers and communities.

4.2.2 Content Marketing

Create valuable and informative content related to interior design, trends, and product guides through blog articles, videos, or podcasts. Optimize your content for search engines to improve the visibility of your website and attract organic traffic. Share your content through social media, newsletters, or guest posting to expand your reach.

4.2.3 Email Marketing

Prepare an email list of interested customers and use email marketing campaigns to generate leads, promote new products, and share exclusive offers or discounts. Personalize your email communication based on customer preferences and purchase history to increase engagement and conversions.

4.2.4 Pay-Per-Click (PPC) Advertising

Make full use of PPC advertising platforms such as Google Ads or social media advertising to reach a your target audience. Develop convincing ad copy and select relevant keywords to ensure your ads are visible to potential customers actively searching for interior products. Observe and optimize your PPC campaigns based on performance metrics to maximize return on investment (ROI).

4.3 Implementing Effective Online Sales and Promotion Strategies

4.3.1 Special Offers and Discounts

Create attractive promotional offers, discounts, or loyalty programs to incentivize online purchases. Highlight limited-time deals or exclusive discounts to create a sense of urgency and bring conversions. Regularly asssess the potency of different promotional strategies and refine them on the basis of consumer response and sales data.

4.3.2 Customer Reviews and Testimonials

Encourage customers to share their feedback and testimonials on your website or third-party platforms. Positive reviews and testimonials build trust and credibility, help potential customers to make purchase decisions in assured manner. Show your commitment to customer satisfaction by responding to their feedback be it negative or positive.

4.3.3 Personalized Recommendations and Upselling

Utilize data analytics and customer segmentation to provide customised product recommendations based on the browsing and purchase history of customers. Apply upselling and cross-selling techniques to encourage customers to explore additional products or upgrade their selections. Customisation can significantly enhance the experience of online shopping and increase the average value of the order.

4.3.4 Influencer Collaborations

Collaborate with interior design influencers or industry experts to promote your products through sponsored content or partnerships. Influencers can help augment your brand's reach, build credibility, and drive traffic to your website. Select influencers whose audience aligns with your target market to ensure maximum impression.

Conclusion

Developing a compelling online presence is vital for interior product retailers to stay competitive and drive revenue growth. By building an engaging and user-friendly website, leveraging social media and digital marketing channels, and implementing effective online sales and promotion strategies, you can expand your reach, attract customers, and increase sales. Regularly monitor and adapt your online strategies based on customer feedback, analytics, and industry trends to ensure your online presence remains relevant and impactful in the ever-evolving digital landscape.

Chapter 5

Implementing Effective Sales & Customer Service Techniques

In the competitive landscape of interior product retail, it is crucial to implement effective sales and customer service techniques in order to drive revenue and build customer loyalty. This chapter will guide you through strategies to train and motivate your sales team, utilize upselling and cross-selling techniques, and enhance customer service to foster loyalty.

5.1 Training and Motivating Your Sales Team

5.1.1 Product Knowledge

Equip your sales team with in-depth knowledge about your interior products. Provide comprehensive training on product features, benefits, and usage scenarios. This will enable your sales team to confidently answer customer inquiries and make well-informed recommendations.

5.1.2 Sales Techniques

Train your sales team on effective sales techniques, including active listening, building rapport, and understanding customer needs. Teach them how to effectively communicate the value of your products and overcome objections. Consistent role-playing exercises and continuous training can help improve their sales skills.

5.1.3 Customer Service Skills

Customer service is an integral part of the sales process. Provide comprehensive training on effective communication, empathy, and problem-solving skills. Encourage your sales team to surpass customer expectations and create a positive shopping experience.

5.1.4 Incentives and Recognition

Motivate your sales team by implementing incentive programs and recognizing their achievements. Offer sales commissions, bonuses, or performance-based rewards to encourage meeting sales targets and goals. Publicly acknowledge exceptional performance through initiatives like employee of the month programs or team recognition events.

5.2 Upselling and Cross-Selling Techniques

5.2.1 Product Knowledge

Ensure that your sales team is well-versed in your product offerings to effectively upsell and cross-sell. Provide training on the benefits and compatibility of different products, enabling your team to assist customers in making well-informed purchasing decisions.

5.2.2 Needs Assessment

Encourage your sales team to engage in a needs assessment conversation with customers. By understanding their specific requirements, your team can recommend complementary products that enhance the customer's purchase or address additional needs.

5.2.3 Bundle Offers

Create bundle offers that combine multiple products at a discounted price. Train your sales team to highlight the value and cost savings of purchasing these bundles, enticing customers to consider upgrading their purchase or adding additional supplementary items.

5.2.4 Upselling Opportunities

Identify upselling opportunities by recommending higher-priced or premium products that align with the customer's needs and preferences. Train your sales team to effectively communicate the additional value and benefits of these products, highlighting their superior quality and enhanced features.

5.3 Enhancing Customer Service and Building Customer Loyalty

5.3.1 Personalized Service

Encourage your sales team to deliver personalized service to each customer. Train them to remember customer preferences, offer tailored recommendations, and follow up after the sale.

Building strong relationships with customers enhances their experience and cultivates loyalty.

5.3.2 Efficient Complaint Resolution

Equip your sales team with the skills to handle customer complaints and issues effectively. Train them to listen actively, empathize with customers, and find satisfactory resolutions promptly. Resolving problems efficiently can turn dissatisfied customers into loyal advocates.

5.3.3 Proactive Communication

Adopt proactive communication strategies to maintain constant connection with customers. Send personalized emails, newsletters, or SMS updates regarding new product arrivals, promotions, or exclusive offers. Regularly engage with customers through social media platforms to address inquiries and build a sense of community.

5.3.4 Customer Loyalty Programs

Implement a customer loyalty program to reward repeat purchases and encourage customer retention. Offer exclusive discounts, VIP access to events, or early product launches as incentives for customers to enroll and actively participate in the program.

Conclusion

In the competitive landscape of interior product retail, it is crucial to implement effective sales and customer service techniques in order to drive revenue and build long-term customer loyalty. By providing comprehensive training and motivation to your sales team, utilizing upselling and cross-selling techniques, and consistently enhancing customer service, you can create a positive shopping experience, boost sales, and foster customer loyalty. Continuously evaluate and refine your sales and customer service strategies based on customer feedback and market trends to ensure your approach remains relevant and effective. Remember, satisfied and loyal customers not only become repeat buyers but also act as advocates for your brand.

Chapter 6

Creating Targeted Marketing Campaigns

To boost revenue and attract customers, it is essential for interior product retailers to develop targeted marketing campaigns that resonate with their specific target market. This chapter will guide you through the process of understanding your target market and buyer personas, crafting compelling marketing messages and promotions, and leveraging data and analytics to optimize your marketing efforts.

6.1 Understanding Your Target Market and Buyer Personas

6.1.1 Market Research

Conduct thorough market research to gain insights into the demographics, preferences, and purchasing behaviour of your target market. Identify trends, market gaps, and customer pain points to effectively tailor your marketing campaigns.

6.1.2 Buyer Personas

Create buyer personas, which are fictional representations of your ideal customers. Define their characteristics, motivations, needs, and challenges. This will enable you to customize your marketing messages and promotions to specific customer segments.

6.1.3 Customer Surveys and Feedback

Regularly gather customer feedback through surveys, interviews, or social media interactions. Understand their preferences, pain points, and expectations to refine your marketing campaigns and provide a personalized experience.

6.2 Crafting Compelling Marketing Messages and Promotions

6.2.1 Unique Selling Proposition (USP)

Identify and articulate your unique selling proposition, which distinguishes your interior products from competitors. Highlight this USP in your marketing messages to convey value and set your brand apart.

6.2.2 Emotional Appeal

Craft marketing messages that evoke emotions and deeply resonate with your target audience. Understand their aspirations, desires, and challenges, and align your messaging to address their needs and offer solutions.

6.2.3 Clear and Concise Communication

Ensure that your marketing messages are clear, concise, and easily comprehensible . Use language that appeals to your target market, avoiding technical jargon or complicated terminology. Focus on highlighting the benefits and outcomes that customers can expect from your products.

6.2.4 Promotional Offers

Create compelling promotional offers that incentivize customers to make a purchase. This can include discounts, limited-time deals, or bundled packages. Clearly communicate the value and urgency of these offers in your marketing campaigns.

6.3 Leveraging Data and Analytics to Optimize Marketing Efforts

6.3.1 Data Tracking and Analysis

Integrate tools and systems to track and analyze marketing data, such as website traffic, conversion rates, and customer engagement. Leverage analytics platforms to gain valuable insights into campaign performance, customer behaviour, and preferences.

6.3.2 A/B Testing

Perform A/B testing to compare different marketing approaches, such as variations in messages, visuals, or call-to-action buttons. Test different elements of your campaigns to identify the most effective strategies and optimize your marketing efforts.

6.3.3 Customer Segmentation

Segment your customer base based on demographics, purchasing behaviour, or engagement levels. Customize your marketing campaigns to address the unique needs and preferences of each segment,, delivering more personalized and relevant messages.

6.3.4 Retargeting and Remarketing

Implement retargeting and remarketing campaigns to reconnect with customers who have previously shown interest in your products. Display targeted ads or personalized offers to re-engage and motivate them to revisit your website or complete a purchase.

Conclusion

Creating targeted marketing campaigns is crucial for interior product retailers to reach their desired audience effectively and drive revenue. By understanding your target market and buyer personas, crafting compelling marketing messages and promotions, and leveraging data and analytics to optimize your efforts, you can create impactful campaigns that resonate with your customers. Continuously monitoring and analyzing campaign performance, adjusting your strategies based on insights gained, and remaining adaptable to changing market dynamics are key to maximizing the effectiveness of your marketing campaigns and achieving your revenue goals.

Chapter 7

Maximizing Customer Engagement & Retention

In order to achieve long-term success, interior product retailers need to prioritize not only on attracting new customers but also maximizing customer engagement and retention. This chapter explores strategies for creating memorable in-store experiences, implementing effective customer loyalty programs, and harnessing the power of reviews and referrals to build a loyal customer base.

7.1 Creating Memorable In-Store Experiences

7.1.1 Store Ambience and Design

Devote attention to your store's ambience and design to create a welcoming and visually appealing environment. Consider factors such as lighting, music, and layout to evoke the desired atmosphere that aligns with your brand image and target market.

7.1.2 Knowledgeable and Friendly Staff

Train your staff to deliver exceptional customer service. Ensure they possess extensive knowledge about your products and can offer expert advice to customers. Encourage friendly and approachable interactions that create a positive and personalized experience.

7.1.3 Interactive Displays and Demo Areas

Incorporate interactive displays and demo areas where customers can actively engage with your products. Allow them to touch, feel, and experience the quality and functionality first-hand. This hands-on approach enhances customer engagement and increases the likelihood of making a purchase.

7.1.4 Engaging Events and Workshops

Organize events, workshops, or design consultations that offer value to your customers. Offer educational sessions, DIY tutorials, or design inspiration to foster a sense of community and position your store as a trusted resource for interior product expertise.

7.2 Implementing Effective Customer Loyalty Programs

7.2.1 Tiered Rewards System

Design a tiered customer loyalty program that offers increasing rewards and benefits as customers advance through different levels. Rewards may include exclusive discounts, early access to new products, or personalized offers customized to their preferences.

7.2.2 Points-Based System

Implement a points-based system where customers earn points for every purchase. These points can be redeemed for discounts, freebies, or other enticing incentives. Clearly communicate the value of the rewards and ensure customers can easily track and redeem their points.

7.2.3 Personalized Communication

Utilize customer data to personalize your communication and offers. Send personalized emails or notifications based on customers' purchase history, preferences, or special occasions. By customizing your messages, you cultivate a feeling of exclusivity and strengthens customer loyalty.

7.2.4 Surprise and Delight

Occasionally, surprise your loyal customers with unexpected rewards or gifts. These unexpected gestures demonstrates appreciation and can substantially elevate customer satisfaction and loyalty.

7.3 Harnessing the Power of Reviews and Referrals

7.3.1 Encouraging Reviews

Motivate customers to share their experiences by urging them to leave reviews and ratings on your website, social media platforms, or third-party review websites. Offer incentives such as discounts or contests to motivate customers to share their experiences. Positive reviews act as social proof and can influence potential customers.

7.3.2 Responding to Feedback

Regularly monitor and respond to customer feedback, whether positive or negative. Express gratitude and appreciation for positive reviews and promptly and professionally address any concerns or issues raised in negative reviews. Demonstrate your dedication to customer satisfaction and continuous improvement.

7.3.3 Referral Programs

Implement a referral program that recognizes and rewards customers for referring their friends or family to your store. Offer incentives such as discounts or store credits to both the referrer and the new customer. Leverage the power of word-of-mouth marketing to expand your customer base.

7.3.4 Influencer Partnerships

Collaborate with influencers or industry experts to showcase your products and create buzz. Collaborating with influencers can provide authentic recommendations and testimonials, attracting their followers and encouraging them to engage with your brand and products.

Conclusion

Maximizing customer engagement and retention is crucial for interior product retailers seeking to build a loyal customer base and drive long-term revenue. By creating memorable in-store experiences, implementing effective customer loyalty programs, and harnessing the power of reviews and referrals. By leveraging these techniques, you can forge strong connections with your customers and keep them coming back. It is essential to continuously evaluate and adapt your strategies based on customer feedback and evolving market trends to ensure your efforts remain relevant and impactful. By prioritizing customer engagement and retention, you can cultivate a thriving and sustainable business.

Chapter 8

Streamlining Operations For Efficiency & Cost Savings

In order to enhance profitability and achieve sustainable growth, interior product retailers need to streamline their operations for improved efficiency and cost savings. This chapter delves into strategies for evaluating and optimizing business processes, implementing measures to enhance inventory and supply chain efficiency, and reducing costs to boost profit margins. By implementing these strategies, retailers can drive operational excellence and position themselves for long-term success.

8.1 Evaluating and Optimizing Business Processes

8.1.1 Process Mapping

Map out your existing business processes to identify areas for improvement and potential bottlenecks. Create a visual representation that illustrates the sequence of activities, inputs, and outputs, allowing you to gain a comprehensive understanding of how your operations function.

8.1.2 Streamlining Workflow

Identify inefficiencies and unnecessary steps within your workflow. Seek opportunities to simplify processes, eliminate redundancies, and automate repetitive tasks. By optimizing your workflow, you can increase productivity and minimize the occurrence of errors or delays.

8.1.3 Technology Integration

Leverage technology solutions to streamline operations. Implement software tools for inventory management, point-of-sale systems, customer relationship management, and data analytics. By automating processes you can save time, improve accuracy, and gain valuable insights to support decision-making.

8.1.4 Continuous Improvement

Establish a culture of continuous improvement within your organization. Encourage employees to contribute ideas for process optimization and achieving efficiency gains. Regularly evaluate and refine your processes based on feedback, data analysis, and industry best practices.

8.2 Implementing Inventory and Supply Chain Efficiency Measures

8.2.1 Demand Forecasting

Utilize historical sales data, market trends, and customer insights to forecast demand with precision. This empowers you to optimize inventory levels, reduce excess stock, and prevent stockouts. Implement inventory management systems that automatically track inventory levels and generate replenishment orders.

8.2.2 Supplier Relationships

Foster collaborative and efficient relationships with suppliers. Negotiate advantageous terms, such as bulk discounts or flexible delivery options. Continuously evaluate supplier performance and explore opportunities for cost savings or process improvement.

8.2.3 Just-in-Time Inventory

Adopt just-in-time (JIT) inventory management practices to minimize inventory holding costs. Align procurement and production processes closely with customer demand to reduce excess inventory and storage expenses. By maintaining optimal inventory levels, you can improve efficiency and maximize cost savings.

8.2.4 Efficient Warehousing and Logistics

Optimize your warehousing and logistics operations for efficiency. Analyze your storage layout, pick-and-pack processes, and transportation routes to minimize time and cost. Embrace technology solutions, such as barcode scanning or warehouse management systems, to streamline operations.

8.3 Reducing Costs and Increasing Profit Margins

8.3.1 Cost Analysis

Conduct a comprehensive analysis of your business costs. Identify areas with high expenditure, such as raw materials, labour, or overhead expenses. Explore opportunities to reduce costs without maintaining product quality or customer satisfaction.

8.3.2 Vendor Negotiations

Negotiate better terms with vendors and suppliers to secure lower prices or volume discounts. Consolidate your purchasing power to negotiate more favourable contracts. Regularly review vendor agreements to ensure competitive pricing.

8.3.3 Energy and Resource Efficiency

Introduce energy-saving initiatives like LED lighting or smart thermostats, to reduce utility costs. Identify ways to minimize waste, promote recycling, and optimize resource consumption. Adopt sustainable practices that align with customer expectations and reduce environmental impact.

8.3.4 Process Automation

Automate manual or repetitive tasks to reduce labour costs and increase productivity. Implement technology solutions that streamline order processing, invoicing, or inventory management. This enables your staff to allocate more time to value-added activities, leading to increased productivity and customer satisfaction.

Conclusion

Streamlining operations for efficiency and cost savings is essential for interior product retailers to improve profitability and stay competitive. By evaluating and optimizing business processes, implementing inventory and supply chain efficiency measures, and reducing costs, you can increase profit margins while maintaining or enhancing customer satisfaction. Continuously monitor key performance indicators, embrace technology solutions, and foster a culture of innovation and continuous improvement. By streamlining operations, you can position your business for long-term success and sustainable growth in the interior product retail industry.

Chapter 9

Analyzing Performance & Making Data-Driven Decisions

In the dynamic and competitive business environment of today, interior product retailers must analyze their performance and make data-driven decisions to maintain a competitive edge. This chapter will delve into strategies for tracking key performance indicators (KPIs), analyzing sales data and customer insights, and utilizing business intelligence tools for effective decision making.

9.1 Tracking Key Performance Indicators (KPIs)

9.1.1 Identifying Relevant KPIs

Identify the KPIs that are most relevant to your interior product retail business. These may include metrics such as sales revenue, profit margin, average order value, customer acquisition cost, customer retention rate, and inventory turnover. Select KPIs that align with your business objectives and provide valuable insights into performance.

9.1.2 Establishing Measurement Systems

Implement systems and tools to accurately track and measure your selected KPIs. This could involve using point-of-sale systems, customer relationship management software, or business intelligence platforms. Automate data collection and reporting processes to streamline the monitoring of KPIs.

9.1.3 Setting Targets and Benchmarks

Set ambitious yet achievable targets for each KPI based on historical performance, industry benchmarks, and growth objectives. Regularly review and revise these targets to align with evolving market conditions and shifting business priorities.

9.2 Analyzing Sales Data and Customer Insights

9.2.1 Sales Data Analysis

Leverage your sales data to gain insights into product performance, customer behaviour, and market trends. Examine sales patterns over time, uncover seasonal peaks or popular products, and discover opportunities for growth and optimization. Segment your sales data by customer demographics, purchase history, or geography to identify patterns and preferences that can inform your business strategies.

9.2.2 Customer Insights

Utilize customer data to gain a deeper understanding of your target audience. Analyze customer demographics, purchasing habits, and preferences to identify valuable segments and tailor your marketing strategies accordingly. Identify customer pain points or areas for improvement through feedback and reviews to enhance customer satisfaction and loyalty.

9.2.3 Predictive Analytics

Leverage predictive analytics tools to forecast sales, customer behaviour, or market trends. Utilize historical data and employ statistical modelling techniques to make informed predictions and anticipate future demand. By leveraging these insights, you can make proactive decisions and allocate your resources effectively to stay ahead in the market.

9.3 Using Business Intelligence Tools for Decision Making

9.3.1 Implementing Business Intelligence (BI) Tools

Invest in robust business intelligence tools that aggregate and visualize data from multiple sources. These tools empower you to create interactive dashboards, reports, and data visualizations that offer a comprehensive overview of your business performance. Utilize BI tools to analyze trends, uncover insights, and make well-informed decisions.

9.3.2 Data-Driven Decision Making

Foster a culture of data-driven decision making throughout your organization. Encourage stakeholders to rely on data and insights when making strategic or operational choices. Base decisions on empirical evidence rather than assumptions, and promote cross-functional collaboration to leverage diverse perspectives.

9.3.3 Scenario Analysis and What-If Modelling

Utilize business intelligence tools to perform scenario analysis and what-if modelling. Test various business scenarios and assess their potential impact on performance and profitability. This helps you evaluate the feasibility and risks associated with various strategies before implementation.

Conclusion

Analyzing performance and making data-driven decisions are crucial for interior product retailers seeking to adapt to market dynamics, optimize operations, and achieve sustainable growth. By diligently tracking relevant KPIs, thoroughly analyzing sales data and customer insights, and effectively utilizing business intelligence tools, you can gain valuable insights into your business performance and make well-informed decisions. It is essential to continuously refine your data collection and analysis processes, stay updated with emerging technologies and industry trends, and prioritize data literacy within your organization. By fully embracing data-driven decision making, you can sharpen your competitive edge and drive success in the interior product retail industry.

Chapter 10

Sustaining Long-Term Growth & Success

To achieve long-term growth and success in the interior product retail industry, it is essential for retailers to develop a strategic approach that adapts to industry trends, evolves with customer needs, and nurture a culture of continuous improvement. This chapter will explore strategies for formulating a long-term growth strategy, embracing industry trends and evolving customer needs, and cultivating a culture of continuous improvement.

10.1 Creating a Long-Term Growth Strategy

10.1.1 Vision and Mission

Define a clear vision and mission statement for your interior product retail business. Clearly communicate the purpose, values, and long-term objectives that guide your strategic decision-making.

10.1.2 Market Analysis

Conduct an in-depth analysis of the interior product retail market, including customer demographics, competition, and emerging trends. Identify growth opportunities, untapped market segments, and areas where your business can differentiate itself.

10.1.3 Goal Setting

Set measurable and achievable goals that align with your long-term growth strategy. These goals should be specific, time-bound, and reflect your desired market position, revenue targets, and customer satisfaction levels.

10.1.4 Diversification and Expansion

Identify possibilities for diversifying and expanding beyond your current product offerings or geographical scope. Evaluate potential strategic partnerships, acquisitions, or entry into new markets as avenues to drive growth and broaden your customer base.

10.2 Adapting to Industry Trends and Evolving Customer Needs

10.2.1 Monitor Industry Trends

Stay abreast of emerging trends in the interior product retail industry. Keep a close eye on evolving consumer preferences, advancements in technology, and emerging design aesthetics. Adapt your product offerings, marketing strategies, and in-store experience to align with these trends.

10.2.2 Customer Research and Feedback

Regularly conduct customer research to understand their evolving needs, preferences, and pain points. Gather feedback through surveys, focus groups, or online reviews to gain insights into areas of improvement. Use this valuable information to refine your product assortment, enhance customer service, and elevate the overall shopping experience.

10.2.3 Omni-channel Strategy

Embrace an omni-channel approach to engage customers across various touchpoints. Seamlessly integrate your brick-and-mortar stores with your online presence, ensuring a cohesive shopping experience across multiple channels. Provide features such as click-and-collect, online ordering, or virtual consultations to cater to customers' diverse preferences.

10.2.4 Sustainable Practices

Address the increasing demand for sustainable and environmentally friendly products. Incorporate eco-friendly materials, promote recycling and upcycling, and communicate your commitment to sustainability to attract conscious consumers.

10.3 Cultivating a Culture of Continuous Improvement

10.3.1 Employee Empowerment

Empower your employees to actively contribute to the success of the business. Encourage them to share ideas for improvement, explore innovative approaches, and provide valuable feedback on existing processes. Foster a culture of innovation and continuous learning, where every individual is invested in the pursuit of improvement.

10.3.2 Training and Development

Invest in the training and development of your employees to enhance their skills and knowledge. Provide ongoing education on industry trends, customer service, sales techniques, and product knowledge. This equips your team with the necessary tools to deliver exceptional service and stay ahead of the competition.

10.3.3 Process Review and Optimization

Regularly review your business processes and identify areas for optimization. Encourage employees to identify bottlenecks, inefficiencies, and opportunities for improvement. Implement a system for continuous process improvement, where feedback is welcomed, and changes are implemented to enhance efficiency and effectiveness.

10.3.4 Innovation and Experimentation

Encourage a culture of innovation and experimentation within your organization. Support and reward employees who generate and implement innovative ideas. Create an environment that embraces calculated risks and views failures as valuable learning experiences for personal and organizational growth.

Conclusion

Sustaining long-term growth and success in the interior product retail industry necessitates a strategic approach that embraces industry trends, caters to evolving customer needs, and fosters a culture of continuous improvement. By developing a comprehensive long-term growth strategy, remaining adaptable to industry trends, and cultivating a culture of continuous improvement, interior product retailers can position themselves for sustainable success in a dynamic marketplace. Regularly reassess your strategies, stay connected with your customers, and embrace change to stay competitive and thrive in the long run.

Conclusion: Achieving & Sustaining Revenue Growth

In the highly competitive landscape of the interior product retail industry, achieving and sustaining revenue growth is a top priority for retailers. By implementing the strategies outlined in this book, retailers can unlock their potential for success and experience a substantial increase in revenue within just 90 days.

Understanding the interior product retail industry is the first step towards success. By analyzing market trends, identifying customer preferences, and staying informed about industry dynamics, retailers can strategically position themselves strategically and make well-informed decisions.

Optimizing product selection and inventory management is crucial for maximizing revenue. By analyzing product performance and profitability, identifying high-demand products and trends, and implementing effective inventory management strategies, retailers can ensure they have the right products in stock and minimize waste.

Enhancing store layout and utilizing visual merchandising plays a vital role in attracting customers and boosting sales. By creating an appealing and customer-friendly store layout, implementing effective visual merchandising techniques, and optimizing product placement and cross-selling opportunities, retailers can create an immersive shopping experience that entices customers to make purchases.

In today's digital age, establishing a compelling online presence is imperative. By building an engaging and user-friendly website, leveraging social media and digital marketing channels, and implementing effective strategies for online sales and promotion, retailers can expand their reach and tap into the vast potential of online shoppers.

Implementing effective sales and customer service techniques is crucial for driving revenue growth. By training and motivating the sales team, utilizing upselling and cross-selling techniques, and enhancing customer service to build loyalty, retailers can increase sales and foster long-term relationships with customers.

Creating targeted marketing campaigns is essential for reaching the right audience and driving sales. By understanding the target market and buyer personas, crafting compelling marketing messages and promotions, and leveraging data and analytics to optimize marketing efforts, retailers can maximize the impact of their marketing campaigns and generate more revenue.

Maximizing customer engagement and retention is a critical factor in driving revenue growth. By creating memorable in-store experiences, implementing effective customer loyalty programs, and harnessing the power of reviews and referrals, retailers can build strong connections with customers, encourage repeat business, and attract new customers through positive word-of-mouth.

Streamlining operations to achieve efficiency and cost savings is essential for maximizing profitability. By evaluating and optimizing business processes, implementing measures to enhance inventory and supply chain efficiency, and reducing costs, retailers can improve operational efficiency, decrease expenses, and increase profit margins.

Analyzing performance and making data-driven decisions are vital for adapting to market dynamics and fostering growth. By monitoring key performance indicators, analyzing sales data and customer insights, and utilizing business intelligence tools for decision-making, retailers can gain valuable insights, identify trends, and make well-informed strategic choices.

Sustaining long-term growth and success necessitates a strategic approach. By developing a long-term growth strategy, adapting to industry trends and evolving customer needs, and cultivating a culture of continuous improvement, retailers can position themselves for ongoing success in the interior product retail industry.

In conclusion, by implementing the strategies and insights shared in this book, interior product retailers can unlock their potential for revenue growth and attain sustainable success. By gaining a deep understanding of the industry, optimizing operations, engaging customers effectively, and leveraging the power of data, retailers can experience significant surges in revenue and establish themselves as leaders in the market. Remember, success is not achieved overnight, but with consistent effort, adaptation, and a customer-centric approach. By embracing these principles, retailers can achieve and maintain revenue growth in the interior product retail industry.

Recap of Key Strategies & Takeaways

Throughout this book, we have explored a range of strategies and techniques aimed at boosting revenue in the interior product retail industry. As a recap, let's review the main strategies and key takeaways from each chapter:

1. Assessing Your Current Business Model:

    a) Evaluate your current revenue streams and identify areas for improvement.

    b) Set revenue goals for the next 90 days to drive growth and measure success.

2. Optimizing Product Selection and Inventory Management:

    a) Analyze product performance and profitability to make informed decisions.

    b) Identify high-demand products and trends to meet customer needs.

    c) Implement effective inventory management strategies to reduce waste and optimize stock levels.

3. Enhancing Store Layout and Visual Merchandising:

   a) Create an appealing and customer-friendly store layout to attract shoppers.

   b) Utilize visual merchandising techniques to highlight products and drive sales.

   c) Optimize product placement and cross-selling opportunities to maximize revenue.

4. Developing a Compelling Online Presence:

   a) Build an engaging and user-friendly website to attract online shoppers.

   b) Leverage social media and digital marketing channels to reach a wider audience.

   c) Implement effective online sales and promotion strategies to drive conversions.

5. Implementing Effective Sales and Customer Service Techniques:

   a) Train and motivate your sales team to increase productivity and customer satisfaction.

   b) Utilize upselling and cross-selling techniques to boost average order value.

   c) Enhance customer service to build loyalty and foster long-term relationships.

6. Creating Targeted Marketing Campaigns:

   a) Understand your target market and buyer personas to tailor your marketing efforts.

   b) Craft compelling marketing messages and promotions to engage customers.

   c) Leverage data and analytics to optimize your marketing strategies and drive results.

7. Maximizing Customer Engagement and Retention:

   a) Create memorable in-store experiences to leave a lasting impression on customers.

   b) Implement effective customer loyalty programs to encourage repeat business.

   c) Harness the power of reviews and referrals to attract new customers through positive word-of-mouth.

8. Streamlining Operations for Efficiency and Cost Savings:

   a) Evaluate and optimize your business processes to increase efficiency.

   b) Implement inventory and supply chain efficiency measures to reduce costs.

   c) Reduce expenses and increase profit margins through smart cost management.

9. Analyzing Performance and Making Data-Driven Decisions:

   a) Track key performance indicators (KPIs) to measure progress and identify areas for improvement.

   b) Analyze sales data and customer insights to gain a deeper understanding of your business.

   c) Utilize business intelligence tools for data analysis and informed decision-making.

10. Sustaining Long-Term Growth and Success:

    a) Create a long-term growth strategy aligned with your vision and mission.

    b) Adapt to industry trends and evolving customer needs to stay relevant.

    c) Cultivate a culture of continuous improvement to drive innovation and growth.

    – By implementing these strategies and capitalizing on the key takeaways, interior product retailers can unleash their potential for revenue growth, thrive in the industry, and achieve sustainable long-term growth. It is important to remember that success demands dedication, continuous learning, and an unwavering commitment to delivering exceptional experiences to your customers.

Encouragement
For Implementing Actionable Steps

Embarking on a journey to boost revenue in your interior product retail business requires more than just acquiring knowledge; it necessitates taking action. As you reflect on the strategies and insights presented in this book, I want to provide you with encouragement and motivation to implement these actionable steps:

1. **Believe in the Potential:** Remind yourself of the incredible possibilities that lie within your business. With the right strategies and effective implementation, you can unlock significant revenue growth. Believe in yourself, your team, and the value you bring to your customers.

2. **Start Small, Aim High:** Taking action can feel overwhelming, especially when confronted with numerous strategies and tasks. To tackle this, break down your goals into smaller, more manageable steps. Begin by focusing on one or two strategies and gradually build momentum. Remember, every small step counts and brings you closer to your revenue objectives.

3. **Embrace Continuous Improvement:** Improving your revenue is a continuous journey. Understand that not every step will be perfect, and errors are an inevitable part of growth. Embrace a mindset of continual improvement and be open to learning from both successes and setbacks.

4. **Build a Supportive Team:** Implementing actionable steps becomes easier when you have a supportive team by your side. Engage your employees, colleagues, or partners in the process. Foster a culture of collaboration, innovation, and shared goals. When everyone is committed to the desired outcome, the likelihood of success increases exponentially.

5. **Celebrate Milestones:** As you make progress and achieve milestones along the way, take the time to celebrate your achievements. Recognize and reward the efforts of yourself and your team. Celebrations not only boost morale but also provide the motivation to keep pushing forward.

6. **Stay Focused and Flexible:** While it's important to stay focused on your revenue growth objectives, also remain flexible in your approach. Adapt to unexpected changes, seize new opportunities, and adjust your strategies as needed. By staying nimble, you can navigate challenges and pivot when necessary.

7. **Seek and Leverage Support:** Don't hesitate to seek support and guidance when needed. Reach out to industry experts, mentors, or professional networks to gain additional insights and perspectives. Collaborate with individuals who have encountered similar challenges and learn from their successes and experiences.

8. **Track and Measure Progress:** Implement tracking mechanisms to monitor your progress. Define key performance indicators (KPIs) that align with your revenue goals and consistently evaluate your performance. This allows you to assess the effectiveness of your strategies, identify areas for improvement, and make data-driven decisions.

9. **Stay Motivated:** Revenue growth requires consistent effort and determination. Stay motivated by reminding yourself of the positive impact these improvements can bring to your business, employees, and customers. Envision the future success you aspire to achieve, and let that vision ignite and propel your drive.

10. **Trust the Process:** Remember that implementing actionable steps takes time. Results may not be immediate, but with patience and persistence, you will start to see the fruits of your labour. Trust the process and stay steadfast on your path towards revenue growth.

A Roadmap To Continued Revenue Growth

Achieving initial revenue growth is an important milestone, but sustaining that growth over the long term is equally crucial for the success of your interior product retail business. To guide you on the path to continued revenue growth, here is a roadmap outlining key steps:

1. **Reflect on Your Successes:** Allocate time for introspection and analyze the strategies and actions that led to your initial revenue growth. Identify the pivotal factors that contributed to your success and understand why they worked. This reflection will serve as a foundation for your continued growth journey.

2. **Set Clear and Measurable Goals:** Define clear and measurable revenue goals for the future. Whether it's a percentage increase in sales, expansion into new markets, or launching new product lines, having specific goals will provide focus and direction for your growth efforts.

3. **Conduct Ongoing Market Research:** Engage in continuous monitoring and analysis of your target market and industry trends. Stay updated on changing

customer preferences, emerging technologies, and competitive landscape. This will enable you to identify new opportunities and adapt your strategies to meet evolving customer needs.

4. **Innovate and Differentiate:** Continued revenue growth necessitates a focus on innovation and differentiation. Continually explore new product offerings, distinctive services, or value-added experiences that set your business apart from competitors. By innovating and staying ahead of the curve, you will attract and retain customers, driving sustained growth.

5. **Expand Your Customer Base:** While maintaining existing customers is important, expanding your customer base is equally vital for continued growth. Develop targeted marketing campaigns to reach new customer segments and tap into previously untapped markets. Leverage digital marketing channels, social media platforms, and customer referrals to broaden your reach.

6. **Foster Customer Loyalty and Advocacy:** Building strong customer loyalty is essential for sustaining revenue growth. Implement customer loyalty programs that incentivize repeat business and provide encourage referrals. Prioritize exceptional customer service and consistently exceed customer expectations to create loyal brand advocates who will support and promote your business.

7. **Invest in Employee Development:** Recognize the crucial role your employees play in driving revenue growth. Invest in their development through training programs, workshops, and continuous learning opportunities. Empower them to deliver exceptional customer experiences and encourage them to contribute innovative ideas that propel growth.

8. **Leverage Technology and Automation:** Explore technology solutions that can streamline your operations, improve efficiency, and enhance customer experiences. Adopt inventory management systems, CRM software, and analytics tools to gain valuable insights and make data-driven decisions. Automation can help optimize processes, reduce errors, and free up resources for revenue-driving activities.

9. **Regularly Evaluate and Adjust Strategies:** Continuously evaluate the effectiveness of your growth strategies and initiatives. Regularly examine key performance indicators, sales metrics, and customer feedback. Identify what's working well and what needs adjustment. Remain open to adaption and modification of your strategies as necessary to ensure progress towards your revenue goals.

10. **Foster a Culture of Continuous Improvement:** Cultivate a culture within your organization that values continuous improvement. Encourage feedback, innovation, and collaboration among your team members. Regularly review and refine processes, seeking opportunities to enhance efficiency and effectiveness. Embrace a growth mindset and constantly seek ways to improve and evolve.

Remember, the road to sustained revenue growth is a continuous journey that demands dedication, adaptability, and a customer-centric approach. By adhering to this roadmap and staying committed to your revenue growth goals, you can navigate obstacles, seize opportunities, and propel your interior product retail business to unprecedented levels of success. Embrace the journey and enjoy the rewards of continued revenue growth and business expansion.

NOTES: